Your 60

Minute

Lean

Business

5S Implementation Guide

D0928911

Your 60 Minute Lean Business
5S Implementation Guide
January 2012
Second Edition

www.lulu.com
ISBN: 978-1-4710-5601-7
Copyright © 2012 Jason Tisbury

Also by Jason Tisbury:

7 Steps To A Lean Business

Pocket Happiness

Contents

Foreword

Welcome to the Lean Business in 60 Minutes series of books. Why 60 minutes? Well for a couple of reasons. It occurred to me a number of years ago while searching through libraries and book stores for texts on the topic of lean manufacturing and lean business that most of the available books were quite large and often not easy to understand for someone new to the topic. The essence of lean is to remove waste from a business and its processes, yet here were all of these books that were filled with non-essential words – waste. I felt a book on the topic of lean should itself be lean. With this in mind I went about writing my first book on lean – 7 Steps To A Lean Business – an overview of lean manufacturing and lean business systems. At 140 pages, this book can be read in a couple of hours and while the details may not enable one to immediately turn a business lean, I believe 7 Steps does provide a very sound overview and ground learning for the lean newcomer.

Now it is time to share the details of some of the different lean tools, I started writing a book detailing all of the tools but soon realised what I was writing wasn't lean enough. And so the Lean Business in 60 Minutes idea was conceived. This book is the first borne from the concept.

If you are a business owner or manager and are looking for a concise, detailed guide to implementing a 5S system, then this book was written especially for you. My goal is to share what I have been lucky enough to learn with other like minded people who may not have had the dumb luck that I have had. When I say dumb luck, I mean dumb luck. The following is the story of how I came to learn lean, I'm sharing this story to firstly build my credentials and secondly to show how anybody can learn and implement these tools.

At the age of 32 I was working in a factory after a recent business failure when I was lucky enough to break two fingers in a ten ton press. It was quite a bad break, twelve months recovery including two surgeries (one bone graft). Now it may seem strange to call that lucky, but luck is what you make of a situation. Even though I had only one working hand, I could still use a computer, and I was fairly handy on a computer (pun not intended). I ended up working with the Quality Manager who by chance was starting to implement some lean manufacturing / continuous improvement ideas in the business. I learnt a great deal during this time. I was also lucky that this company was in the automotive industry and that one of their main customers was Toyota, probably the best company in the world to learn from. I spent the next five years living and breathing the Toyota Production System (TPS) with direct instruction and mentoring through Toyota. Now after having implemented lean systems and tools through a variety of companies in many organisations in many diverse industries, it is time to share what I have learnt for others to benefit.

What is 5S

5S plays a big part in any lean manufacturing system. You will see in this guide that it is much more than just a housekeeping program. The 5S's stand for Seiri, Seiton, Seiso, Seiketsu, Shitsuke. Translated these are Sort, Set in Order, Shine (sometimes called Sweep), Standardise and Sustain. There is often a 6th S added – this is usually Safety.

5S is often referred to as a housekeeping program, beware of anyone doing this – it shows either a lack of understanding of 5S or a lack of belief. The benefits of 5S are discussed in the next section, but at this point I will say they go much deeper than housekeeping.

5S is one of the foundation stones of any lean system, without 5S in place all other improvements will be very difficult to sustain. The lean house is a symbolic building diagram showing the different tools and principles of lean or TPS and how they fit together in the building structure. 5S is one of the foundation stones. The lean house diagram can be seen on the next page.

So the best way to describe a 5S system is to call it "A system to ensure the workplace enables effective and efficient outputs". Yes this is a bit of a quality managers terminology, I won't apologise for that. It isn't a coincidence that continuous improvement is a major factor in ISO 9001 and TS16949 – it really does work and improved quality is just one of the benefits.

Lean Business

Jidoka – Quality

Just In Time

Standardised Work

Kaizen

5S

TPM

8

Benefits

As I mentioned earlier, the benefits of 5S are far greater than simply improved housekeeping. A sustained 5S system will bring the following benefits:

- Improved safety

- Improved quality

- Increased efficiency

- Improved customer satisfaction

- Reduced operating costs

- Reduced material waste

- Improved staff morale and happiness

- Improved team work

This list will be very similar for each of the lean tools and principles, how much of a difference will vary with the different tools but I think you get my point. 5S is much more than a housekeeping program.

The main benefits 5S will provide are detailed below.

Improved safety

By maintaining a workplace where everything is in the correct place the hazards will be greatly reduced. Walkways will be clearer and working areas will be cleaner. Operators will have less walking during their day to day work due to required parts and tools being close at hand.

Improved Quality

By only having the right parts at hand, the likelihood of incorrect processing are reduced. When the correct tools are provided for the operator the chances of damaging the product through incorrect technique are reduced.

Increased efficiency

With reduced walking comes increased efficiency. Having every part and tool in the right place means less searching – this equates to improved efficiency.

Improved customer satisfaction

With improved quality and efficiency your customers will be happier with you. Simple as that really.

Reduced operating costs

Reducing your defects, improving efficiency and improving safety will al lead to reduced operating costs. Reduced operating costs mean increased profits. You've got to love that idea.

Reduced material waste

When you improve quality you do so by reducing the frequency of defects. Every time a defect occurs your material costs increase. Lower defects equals reduced material waste. Can you see the trend here? It's like compounding interest; the benefit to effort ratio increases.

Improved staff morale and happiness

No-one enjoys working in untidy or unsafe conditions. No-one enjoys making mistakes or working inefficiently. By enabling your employees to work in a safer, cleaner environment with fewer defects your staff will be happier, healthier and more loyal.

Improved team work

If you follow this guide, every employee in your organisation will have a role to play in implementing the program and realising the benefits. Every time you are undergoing a project in the factory, warehouse or office make sure a cross section of the business is involved – in the factory; have people from the warehouse and office involved and visa versa. This will not only promote team work but will also build strong relationships.

In overview, the benefits your business can realise through the implementation and maintenance of an effective 5S program are substantially more than the outlay required. By following this guide anyone can implement an effective program.

5S in 60 Minutes

Step One -
Before You Begin

There are a few prerequisites that need to be in place and followed. Without some of these prerequisites success will be difficult at best, without others, success is still very achievable; I think you will be able to identify which are the most important.

Buy-in

This may seem obvious however it requires discussion. It is critical that you have the buy-in from two different groups within your business.

The first group is the executive management / business owners. You will need to have the buy-in and support of this group to firstly drive the changes at their level, without this buy-in it is highly likely that you will spend a large portion of your time justifying your program. You will also need their commitment to gain approval for any capital and/or overhead expenses.

The second group you will need the buy-in from is from the target work area. This can be a factory, warehouse or office area; whatever the work area, you will need to have the buy-in from the team.

Buy-in or ownership is critically important in any change program. It will make or break your success in implementing a sustainable 5S culture. You can achieve some small and not so small improvements without full buy-in however, you will struggle to achieve the great successes you can with it.

Defined Area

As I said above, the selected area can be from anywhere in the business. Saying this, I have always found it best if the initial test area is within a factory or warehouse environment. Depending on your business these areas will be where your business makes its money – make a good improvement here and you will likely realise a financial benefit (this can be very important early in the lean journey). The important thing at this point is that the area chosen is quite small and contained. Whether this is the first time a 5S program has been run in the business or this is the final area to undertake the change, it is a good idea to limit the size of the area in the program. There is no limit to the number of target 5S areas you can have in the business, actually it is almost a case of the more the better.

So, we have chosen a small work area, what's next?

Defined Teams

When you get into the work area, you'll need small teams to work together during various stages of the process. These teams should include at least one person NOT from the working area whenever possible. The reason for this is to bring 'fresh eyes' to the team. A fresh set of eyes will often 'see' opportunities that are missed by those working within the area as it is natural to become blind to normality.

Selection of the teams is an important step and should be done to enable the teams to achieve the best outcomes possible. Each team needs to have a leader – even if you choose to not designate a leader, a natural leader needs to be present to maintain the focus.

You may identify people in your group that are not 'team players' – these people need to be placed in teams that have the capacity to drive effectiveness from every team member and a strong leader or leadership group to ensure this team member is kept in line. Don't give these people an easy ride they need to go into a team that will manage this well – you may find this team needs to be led by a supervisor or manager; maybe even yourself.

Make sure the teams have clearly defined targets and areas of responsibility. Remember, what gets measured, gets managed!

Budget and Authority

It may be difficult for your first program, but a small budget will make the process more streamlined and will help achieve greater early success. There will be small items that need to be purchased during the first two stages; if you are able to purchase these without waiting for approval you will not only have faster success, but it will also help with buy-in from the team.

You need to ensure you have some authority from the business to make relevant decisions during the program. Most of these decisions will be small and will have little or no impact on the running of the business.

Current State Photographs

Before you begin making any changes it is a very good idea to take photographs of the current situation. It is very easy to forget where you have come from once the changes have been made. They say a picture paints a thousand words – well that is only true if it is the right picture. So how do you take the right picture?

- Find a good vantage point to get the best perspective for your photograph

- Mark or identify the spot the photograph is taken from

- Take before and after photographs from the same location to increase the visual impact your photographs make

- Take as many photographs as you can at both the before and after stage. With digital cameras you can afford to take plenty and discard those that are not suitable for use

We're about to get into the 5S steps, but before we do, if you are very new to 5S and lean manufacturing you may want to jump to Appendix C and take a quick look at the tools and training materials section. Bookmark the pages so you can easily flick to learn more about the specific tools as needed.

Step Two
Sort

Aim:

The aim of this step is to remove anything from the area that should not be there. The first thing we need to do here is to define "what shouldn't be in the area".

A good way to define this is:

Usage / Value	Disposition
Junk , no value	Rubbish
Excess consumables	Return to store
Not needed	Red Tag area
Daily usage	Visible and accessible
Weekly usage	Store in work area
Monthly usage	Store centrally / return to stores
Less than monthly	Return to stores or store outside work area

This is a guide only and it should be tailored to your work environment and infrastructure. It does provide a starting point though. With these guidelines in place let's get started with sorting.

What you'll need.

- A 5S Red Tag area (this area will be discussed shortly).

- Red Tags (optional) - these are available online or you can make your own.

- Good understanding of tool requirements to undertake the work in the area.

- Red Tag register (optional) – used to record all items removed to the red tag area and later removed from the area. This can be handy in case someone asks for something at a later date.

- Blank 5S requirement work sheet (optional).

How:

Now the fun begins, start working through the area in teams of two or three people – as defined earlier. Remember in this step all you are doing is sorting what should and shouldn't be in the area. Each team should be armed with red tags and a red tag register.

- As an item is identified as not being required for use in the area, attached a red tag and populate the red tag register. The red tags should be numbered to enable easier identification later.

- Remove the item to the designated red tag area. All of these items will be analysed closely later.

- Be brutal! Everything in doubt should be removed to the red tag area during this phase. Have the discussion later.

This should be one of the fastest phases of the entire program. If you find your team is taking too long to discuss items as they go you should intervene. Any discussion should be held during the next phase of the sorting step.

Ask this question "When will this item be used?" If the answer is unknown or is greater than a week then remove it from the area and attach a red tag. If the answer cannot be agreed upon or takes an unreasonable amount of time to answer then remove it from the area and attach a red tag.

After sorting through the area you will have only the tools required to do the job at hand in the area and a red tag area with a large number of tagged items. If the quantity of items in the red tag area is small then either you were not brutal enough or your area was reasonably well kept beforehand.

The red tag area needs to be in a position that can be left for at least a couple of days without creating any issues. If you can organise racks in the area this will help to better organize things. The red tag area needs to be clearly defined and identified and should be partitioned off from the work areas.

Now you have to hold off on doing anything. Let the work in the area carry on as usual for two to three days. This will either a) reinforce that the removed items are not required in the work area or b) force the retrieval of some of the items from the red tag area. It really doesn't matter which of these two occur as this is just confirming the sort.

Do not discourage the retrieval of items as long as they are used for their designed purpose. What does this mean exactly? If they retrieve a screwdriver to scrape paint for example then this should not be retrieved as it not being used for the designed purpose. In this instance, a paint scraper will be added to the 5S requirements work sheet and later purchased once approved.

The next action is to conduct an auction for the items in the red tag area. Many practitioners conduct the auction shortly after removing the items, in my experience this will result in many of the unnecessary items being 'bought' back by the users. By taking two to three days to a week before conducting the auction, the users will now be used to operating without the items.

The auction should take place within the red tag area and should be conducted by the area team leader, supervisor or manager to make it more interesting.

- Each item is raised for the auction in turn.

- Rather than auctioning for a price, a bidder need only raise their hand to 'purchase' the item.

- The only rule here is they must have a better than good reason for needing the item.

When an item is returned to the work area, monitor the use of the item over a period of time to ensure the excess tools do not begin to build up again. This sorting process can be performed at a regular interval – annually is a good start. Any more than this and you will be over analysing and less frequent and you could come back to quite a big task again.

All items in the red tag area need to have a disposition. Whether the item is returned to the work area, is moved into storage/warehouse, is relocated to another work area or is scrapped, every item must be dealt with.

After the initial sort, you shouldn't need to have a great deal of input into future sort exercises. It is important with any of the lean tools (as with other business tools) that the tools become ingrained into the day to day operations of the business – this means every employee has a responsibility to incorporate the tools into their daily work. Small actions repeated and built upon over a period of time make a big impact.

Sort Guidelines

- Every item in the area needs to be analysed for requirement and usage frequency

- Set up your red tag area

- Remove all unused items to the red tag area

- Wait

- Hold your auction

- Make sure a solid argument exists for the return of any items

Step Three
Set in order

Aim:

The aim of this step is to ensure every item needed in the area has a home – A place for everything and everything in its place.

What you'll need:

- The completed 5S requirements work sheet
- Current 5S Audit results

How:

Setting in order should be started soon after the sort has been completed and the red tag auction is complete. The longer the wait between steps, the more likely you will need to sort again before applying the set in order phase. Basically, this is about making the items easily accessible every time to improve efficiency and reduce quality issues and costs (through replacements and efficiency). What does setting in order apply to? In short, it applies to everything:

- OHS information and equipment
- Tools
- Inventory items
  - Raw materials – in an office this could be inputs to your business process
  - Sub-assemblies
  - Consumables

- Work instructions

- Work schedules

- Samples

- Quality inspection equipment and information

- Reporting documents and tools

- Contact details and system for supervisors

If you have a floor plan on CAD it will make your life easier, otherwise you will need to sketch out the work space. Earlier I mentioned the good practice of working in a small area for each project. This is when you will understand why it is good practice. There are a couple of reasons for this:

- A smaller area can be set in order in a shorter amount of time

- The cost to complete the set in order of a smaller area is far less than that of a larger work area. This cost takes into account both material and labour

- The benefits will be realised sooner, this will help with momentum for the next areas and also help with buy-in from all parties. Once management see the results that can be achieved through the sorting and setting in order of a small area, they will be more supportive of future projects.

Back to sketching the work area, if you have a CAD diagram of the work area even better, but there is nothing wrong with sketching. A pencil sketch will be ok to get you started, but it is a good idea to follow this up with a drawing at least close to scale. This drawing is of the current state and should show as near everything as possible. Before you start to amend the layout, take a couple of copies of the raw sketch – this will save you time later when you want to make revisions.

Next you will need the completed 5S requirements sheet and a full list of all of the items used in the area. This list needs to include:

- Raw materials
- Components
- Tools
- Equipment
- Work area
- Inspection equipment
- Inspection work area
- Housekeeping equipment

Before moving on I am going to digress a little and discuss the Plan Do Check Act (PDCA) cycle. Although the PDCA cycle is often referred to as a quality tool, it has a big part to play lean systems also and is very useful in the set in order stage.

Let's go through the PDCA cycle one step at a time.

The process always begins with planning. This step usually takes up to 2/3 of the project timing. As you read this book you will notice that the 7 steps of this book are based on this cycle. The first two chapters would be included in the Planning stage. This chapter and the next are also both in the planning stage (some parts of chapter 4 are also in the Do stage as will be explained later).

Plan – Analyse what has gone wrong? Find a gap and make a plan to implement countermeasures.

Do – Trial the countermeasure.

Check – Measure the outcomes from the trial to determine the effectiveness.

Act – If the countermeasures provide the desired outcomes – implement on a larger scale and share the lessons learnt. Otherwise develop new countermeasures and return to "Do".

Now we all understand the PDCA cycle, we have to begin the planning of how we will set in order. Just as items that are used frequently are kept within the area, items with the highest frequency usage should be located nearest the user. Further to this there are some good guidelines on workspace ergonomics that can be easily found on the internet; incorporating better Occupational Health & Safety into the layout is a must have. As a general rule, try to limit the amount of movement (particularly twisting and reaching) of the person to reduce the risk of injury and to also improve efficiency.

You will need to draw a revised or future layout for the overall area. This will look at thoroughfares, work flow, material flow and bulk storage options. You are likely to need a number of versions of the future layout, these should not be undertaken by a single person, but should be completed with the input of the entire team. Once you have a number of options drafted, it is time to gain consensus for a single option; a combination of different options can come together to provide a new alternative.

The next step is to draft up the macro work stations within the work area. Hopefully you have taken heed and are working on a relatively small area. You will need to follow the same process as you did with the work area; drafting a few versions and gaining consensus etc.

These two future maps must incorporate storage for every item you listed on both the 5S requirements sheet and the list of items used in the area. Once you have the two plans drafted you will need to put together an action plan of every item and the step by step program of how they will be implemented.

One of the first action items should be to apply a cost to the changes and build a business case to gain approval for the capital expenditure. Even if the costs are negligible or your business does not require you to go to this extent, I would implore you to undertake this activity and report the costs and the benefits to your superiors. By doing so, you are showing your own commitment and belief in the 5S process; this should build more buy in from the entire business.

To gain approval for your implementation you will need to show a return on the investment (ROI). This is another reason why you should start with a smaller work area – to keep the capital expenditure down. One of the first and best things I was taught from Toyota training is that some of the best ideas are often not expensive or are even free to implement (excluding of labour costs). Don't dismiss an idea just because it doesn't cost a lot to implement, at the same time you shouldn't dismiss an idea just because it costs too much for implementation. It all comes down to ROI. To calculate the ROI, it is a simple process of first understanding your costs, then translating these costs into time. Next calculate the savings the changes can bring to the process and then translate these savings into time.

For example:

If the cost of the changes is $15,000 and the savings are $1,000 per week then your ROI is 15 weeks. If the cost is $50,000 and the savings are $800 per week then the ROI is 63 weeks.

As a general rule of thumb, if you have a project with an ROI of less than one year then you should really try and implement it.

Another good way to measure ideas is by using a cost benefit matrix / chart. This is a simple two axis scale. The X axis is for benefit; the Y axis is for cost. Ideas are placed on the chart according to where they sit in relation to the cost and potential benefits. As in the above ROI calculation, the lower cost and higher benefit ideas are where you should start. A common alternative is a four quadrant graph with:

Quadrant 1 – Low Cost/High Benefit

Quadrant 2 – Low Cost/Low Benefit

Quadrant 3 – High Cost/High Benefit

Quadrant 4 – High Cost/Low Benefit

The place to start with this method is Q1, then move onto Q2/Q3 and then stop. There is no point in moving onto the Q4 ideas. You probably wouldn't even implement all of the Q2 and Q3 ideas. You can also add 'Time to implement' to the cost scale and 'Ease of implementation' to the benefits scale; this can give you a fuller analysis by not restricting you to monetary values only.

Once you have the above analysis you can go about gaining approval for financial support. While you are going through the above it is a good idea to "Do" some of the items in a trial. If you wait until financial approval you will lose too much time and also run the risk of requesting capital that is not required while also missing other capital items as the requirements change through the trialing stage. This is the "Do" step in the PDCA cycle and is a critical step in achieving success. Some items cannot be trialed until the approval is gained due to machinery or tooling requirements, however there are usually many that can be trialed.

This will enable you to fine tune the concepts before final implementation. This fine tuning step is the "Check" step in the PDCA cycle. This is where most businesses projects fail. Anyone can have an idea and go and put the idea into practice, however to turn an idea into a sustainable improvement you need to "check" that it is working as planned and that it is realising the planned (or desired) benefits. The checking stage needs to be structured to ensure what you measure can be used for deeper analysis. In a similar method to a scientific experiment, you need to set the scope of the trial, closely measure and accurately record the outcomes. In reality, the "Do" and "Check" steps are performed simultaneously.

By following these steps you can then "Act" by implementing the final process and layout without excessive modification or difficulty. Some of the main points are below:

- Get the entire team involved in development of the layout and process

- Get buy-in from the business early in the project

- Follow the PDCA cycle to give your project the best chance of success

- Work on a small area at a time

- Complete the Set In Order for each small area before moving onto the next area

- Every item (tools, inventory, inspection etc) must have a home once this step is complete

Step Four
Shine

Aim:

The aim of this step is to clean the surfaces, equipment and tools to enable fast identification of a problem.

What you'll need:

- Cleaning equipment
- Tooling / plant operating and maintenance instructions

How:

This could be a small chapter! What we are doing is cleaning, but it really is a lot more than just cleaning. Like every other activity their needs to be plan, and the plan is structured around the PDCA cycle.

Question:

What are you going to clean?

Answer:

In short, everything in the area. To really understand the answer to this question we must explore another question. We can then return to this answer.

Question:

Why are we cleaning?

Answer:

There can be many reasons we should perform the cleaning step in the 5S program. The first is to ensure we are starting our journey from the best position. If we ignore this step then we will never really see the work area as good as it could be. Therefore we will be starting off from a poor position and will never reach our ultimate goal. If we follow the Shine step, we will set a high standard, this will be discussed more in the next chapter – Step 5 Standardise.

Another and the main reason for following this step is to provide the best operating environment for machinery and plant. Only with this environment in place will you be in a position to identify an issue with the equipment early enough to rectify the problem before it becomes critical. If this environment is not in place it is quite likely the first you know of a problem is when it is too late – either a defect has been passed on to the customer or the equipment has broken down and has caused unplanned downtime.

Now back to the first question; the short answer was we clean everything. In reality we need to clean more than everything. Impossible I know, but it needs to be made clear just how far the cleaning needs to go. Clean everything you think needs cleaning, and then look further for more cleaning opportunities.

Start by cleaning the general floor area, sweeping the floor, then follow with an industrial cleaning system if possible. Next you should clean all machinery, tables, benches and racking. Every surface area needs to be cleaned at this initial stage. The machinery needs to be treated even further.

- All guarding is removed and cleaned

- All oil marks and leaks are cleaned

- All leaks need to be repaired where practical

- Under machines should be cleaned

This may seem like a lot of effort for not a lot of gain, but it is very important this step is followed as you will soon realise the benefits of the initial clean. This will positively impact:

- Team morale

- Product quality

- Operating efficiency

- DIFOT (Delivery In Full On Time)

- Customer satisfaction

- Profitability

The Big Clean:

Every one has had some exposure to cleaning I'm sure, some much more than others – depending on how we grew up I guess, so there shouldn't be a great need for too much instruction, however I will say the best method I have found is to divide and conquer.

Divide the work area into smaller areas on the layout and assign a responsible person or team (teams will be more effective) to clean each of these smaller areas. After the clean inspection of the areas needs to be performed; this can be by the facilitator, a manager / supervisor or by cross checking by the cleaning team. The latter can be very effective when the teams are competitive and have bought into the process. Only when the cleaning is complete has the Shine step been completed – remember to set expectations prior to the commencement.

After all the cleaning is complete and the inspectors are satisfied it is time for a team walk to verify the standards have been met. Get the entire team together and walk slowly through the work area. The facilitator or manager need to be the 'guide' through the walk. Be very critical (but practical) through this step, this is a chance for the expectations to be set, reinforced and understood.

Once there is full agreement that the shine is at acceptable levels you can move onto the next step.

Step 5
Standardise

Aim:

The purpose of this step is to make the work practices and flow consistent from station to station. Any sufficiently skilled person should be able to work at any work station and locate the tools and parts to do the job.

How:

This step is the one that causes the most backward sliding in businesses. The first two or three steps are quite active and therefore rewards are realised quickly. This step is less activity based.

There are a couple of distinct ways to look at the standardising step. The first looks at turning the new work area into the "standard" – in effect following the ISO 9001 rule of clearly defining standards to be achieved. The second is to standardise the work stations throughout the work-centre and greater business – this will enable any person from any area to more easily work in a different work area.

Let's begin by looking at the first definition. Hopefully you followed the instructions in Step One and have taken some "Before" photographs. Now is when you can use them. Print out some good (bad) examples of how the work area was before the first 3S's. Take these printouts to the work area and take some new photographs to show the changes and new work area after the work has been performed. It is important now to take the after photographs from the same aspect and angle as the before photographs. It is a good idea to create a map early on and mark where the before shots were taken.

Once the photographs have been taken successfully, we can build a 5S storyboard. A magnetic whiteboard will be ideal for this purpose. If you have an 1800x1200mm whiteboard you can use half for the storyboard. A photograph of the team can be placed on the top of the storyboard next to the title. This should include all members of the team that work in the area and who were involved in the project. If you had a person who was uncooperative ad was not involved in the project they can be left out of the photograph. Conversely if you had a person who was uncooperative but was involved reluctantly, this person should be included in the photograph.

What you'll need to create the storyboard:

- 1800x1200mm magnetic whiteboard
- Before photographs
- After photographs
- Team photograph
- Permanent markers or whiteboard tape

- Lamination pouches
- Magnetic clips or magnets
- Headings / notes etc – laminated
- Large coloured arrows - laminated

Divide the board in half with the permanent marker or whiteboard tape (the other half will be used in the next chapter). You can layout your storyboard however you prefer, the following is how mine are laid out – I always try to keep them to a standardized layout.

- Position your main header centred at the top
- Place your team photo to the left of the heading
- Position all of your "before" photo's on the left
- Position arrows to the right of the before photo's
- Position "after" photo's to the right of the arrows
- Position any notes or descriptions directly to the right of the photographs

Some things to keep in mind:
- Less is often more
    o Try not to clutter the board
- Make sure the layout "tells a story" and isn't just pictures on a board
- Make the photo's as large as practical to enable easy viewing

It's quite important that the board is actually handed over to the 5S team at this time. This is why the team photograph is added to the board – to promote ownership and responsibility. Even without going to the next level this storyboard should provide some level of responsibility to maintain the new current state.

The "after" images will set in stone the new minimum standard for housekeeping in this area. At this point you should bring other team leaders, supervisors and managers through the area to showcase the work that has been undertaken. Have the team members talk about the changes and tell the story through the storyboard. This will further promote ownership and increase pride in the area. Promote the area through tool-box meetings, management meetings etc. to heighten the profile throughout the business.

Celebrate with the team! I know we are now only 4/5ths through the process, but the 5th step is very much driven by the facilitator or manager and not the shop floor. So now is the time to celebrate; it can be small or big – depending on the project itself. Whatever you choose, you need to celebrate; this is an absolute must in every change project and is a pivotal step in any change management system.

Now to the second definition: to standardise the work stations and work areas throughout the work centre and greater business. This definition will bring far greater gains than the first definition however will also be a longer and more involved process requiring great commitment. The benefits you will realise by following this step can turn your business into a world class performer! Yes it really is that powerful. And the best news is that the hard work has already been done. By creating a benchmark area in your business you have proven that 5S works, is achievable and provides tangible benefits to the organisation.

The first thing you want to do is standardise the workstations within the work area. Once again, earlier I said to make sure the initial trial area was small, well now you can expand on that and spread the 5S word. Only now you and your team have the added benefit of what you have already learned through your initial trial area.

Depending on your workplace, this may be as simple as copying the work you have already done in the trial area. However it may be necessary and it is highly advisable to follow all of the steps again. By doing this you will ensure the best results and eliminate complacency. Remember, to become a lean business takes planning and effort – there are no shortcuts.

Once you have worked your way through the work area, you should further standardise throughout the rest of the business. Obviously, the further you move away from the initial trial area, the more important it becomes to closely follow the preceding steps. This can process can be just as effective in a manufacturing environment or an office environment.

Upon the completion of this step you should have a business that is operating with a high level of 5S. This will create a strong foundation for further continuous improvement initiatives.

Before moving on to the next chapter, I think it is important to briefly discuss the meaning of "standardised". It can be easy to become too focused on standardising to make all work centre's very similar. While this may be close to the true definition of the word; in the context of lean manufacturing and quality management this will hinder your progress. In the context we require; by standardising we are copying the process and resultant best practice work area. In essence we are following a standardised process to achieve an outcome which is to a required standard or level to enable the required tasks to be performed in the most efficient and effective manner.

Step 6
Sustain

Aim:

The aim of this step should be quite clear from the title: to sustain the progress made through the 5S program.

How:

The implementation of a sustainable 5S system is the obvious desired outcome from a 5S program. Unfortunately, as mentioned earlier in this book, most businesses embarking on the journey never achieve it. Most will work through to setting in order (and do this step quite well) before losing momentum. This then becomes a sort, set in order, begin shine, other priorities, sort ... you get the idea. You need to make sure this does not become you.

Ideally you will follow this step with standardising across the business as discussed in the previous chapter.

According to dictionary.com sustain means "to keep up or keep going, as an action or process". So it is pretty obvious that by sustaining our 5S program we are looking to ensure it keeps going. Sounds easy right? Well it can be, if done right.

There are really two ways to sustain any business process both are easy in different ways and both are difficult in different ways.

Manually

This method works by management enforcing the continual maintenance of the new system. This can be achieved with a few methods:

- Linking all system requirements to position descriptions
- Involve management in layered audits
- Linking audit results to position description and or bonus schemes
- Layered reporting of audit results and program outcomes

The list here could be very long but I think you should get the drift from this list. All of these methods will work to some extent by themselves, however to get the best results you can combine more than one or even all of them.

Pros

Some of the pros of using this type of system to sustain your 5S program are:

- Management involvement

- Through layered audits, management will be forced to "walk the Gemba" – place of value adding. Walking the Gemba can also be known as Genchi Genbutsu – "Go and see"

- High accountability from team members

- Hierarchal ownership of the new system

- While the accountability is measured, the system is highly likely to be upheld

Cons

Some of the cons of using this type of system are:

- Reliance on enforcement for system success

- Lack of true ownership by the team

- Lack of drive from the team members can result in ad hoc system compliance
  - System may appear sustained during times of review or audits, however in normal practice may be non compliant
  - This is due to "enforced compliance" by management. This can be more of an issue when weak bonus schemes are applied (for more info see appendix)

Auto / Embedded

This method relies on strong change management skills by the facilitator / facilitation team to create a powerful sense of ownership within the team. This can be achieved by using some of the following techniques:

- Continuous communication between management and the team
    - Communication must be open, honest and cyclical
- Team involvement throughout the program
    - This has been discussed in earlier chapters, however cannot be underestimated
- Management involvement in activities
    - Management involvement can help create greater connection, trust and communication between management and team members

Pros

Some of the pros of using this system are:

- True ownership by the team
- Team driven improvements
- Low reliance on management to drive further improvements
- Empowerment of workforce
- Better integration between workforce and management
    - This can have a long term positive impact on organisational internal harmony
    - Reduce potential for labour disputes

- System involvement is managed by team members

Cons

Some of the cons of using this system are:

- Potential for reduced management involvement post activities
  - This can reduce some of the positives from above
- It is possible for some teams to lose direction without involvement from managers
  - Some team members just will not accept empowerment or ownership of a process
  - Although this is a rarity, to ignore it would be negligence on my part

From this list of pros and cons the only certainty is they are both viable options – both bring very different benefits to the process. These benefits cannot be underestimated. How you go about this step of your 5S program will have the greatest impact on future improvement projects in the organisation. If this step is implemented in a structured and measured way your chances of success will be greatly improved.

Just as in every previous step, by following the PDCA cycle through this stage you will follow a structured, focused and planned method to achieving sustainability. I would recommend using a combination of both options to achieve the best result with maximum benefits.

Sustaining your program does not start at this step; in reality it starts way back at the beginning. By achieving good buy-in from all stake holders from the outset, you can now call up that ownership from management and team members alike. If you were able to achieve good buy-in this step will not be at all difficult – however, if you received only superficial buy-in then you could be in for a challenge. Early planning (with the PDCA cycle) will also make this task easier.

So how are we going to sustain your 5S program? There are a few steps that can be taken to ensure sustainability.

1. Develop a 5S audit sheet

    1.1. Templates can be downloaded from many websites for free. Visit www.lean-learnings.com to download one example.

    1.2. Conduct audits daily by the team members initially. This can later be reduced to weekly once the system is well sustained

        1.2.1. Make every team member responsible for something on the audit sheet

    1.3. Display the audit sheet on the 5S storyboard

        1.3.1. This is where you can use the spare half of the board discussed earlier

    1.4. Graph the weekly results on a web diagram

    1.5. Record the results in a spreadsheet – these results can be graphed to show improvements or declines over time with trends

2. Run a layered audit program

    2.1. Begin with the team leaders and supervisors conducting a weekly audit

2.2. Production management, Quality & HR should perform a monthly audit

    2.2.1. This can be rotated through the different managers

2.3. A quarterly audit should be performed by senior management

    2.3.1. Once again, this can be on a rotational schedule

3. Results from all audits should be displayed on the 5S Storyboard alongside graphs showing trends

4. Results also should be reported and discussed as part of any management reporting system

5. Site visitors should be sought after – show off the work you have done

6. Encourage other departments to implement their own 5S program

    6.1. Run competitions between departments to drive further improvements and instill a sense of pride in the teams.

7. Push – keep driving the 5S culture throughout the organisation

    7.1. There will be times when you feel like you are the only one pushing, but it is critical for the program success that you maintain the push

Remember, this will not happen by itself, anything worthwhile needs commitment and persistence. A 5S program is for a business what a success system (from The Success System That Never Fails - W. Clement Stone) is for personal success. In the book The Greatest Secret In The World, Og Mandino introduced the Success Recorder- this is also discussed in The

Success System That Never Fails. The 5S audit sheets used in this step of your program are the organisations 5S Success Recorder. These documents and the associated charts and graphs will enable you to easily monitor the performance of both the teams involved and the organisation in general.

Step 7
Start over

The 5S's are a small part of a Continuous Improvement Plan or Strategy. As the name suggests Continuous Improvement is an ongoing process, it is a never ending cycle that is followed in the pursuit of the future state plan. More on this is the Lean in 60 Minutes book – Lean Philosophy/Strategy.

Being an ongoing process, it is important to revisit the 5S areas routinely. There are a couple of ways to do this.

You can run your 5S program through the entire organisation once. This will usually start with the manufacturing, logistics and through to the offices and management areas of the business. This process will take many months to complete – possibly years. Once the cycle of the business is complete you can start over; by doing so you will be using skills you have now honed through many months of exercising. This second and subsequent implementations will be faster and much more productive than the first attempt. The downfall to this method is the time between the initial and subsequent implementations of the same area, which will likely be months, possibly years.

Alternatively, you can structure your 5S program to run systematically during the sustaining stage. In addition to the audit and reporting schedule you can easily set up a revisit schedule. By running the red tagging and auction regularly – every three to six months works well – you will further ensure the success of your program. This will also further instill the culture change and the empowerment within the team – more on culture change in Appendix B.

It is important these planned 5S programs are discussed with the teams throughout the process – right from the early meetings. This will not only help overcome any last minute protests against the routine programs but will also reinforce the ownership of the tools from an early point in the journey. These points have been stressed a lot in this book; this is for the simple reason that they are so important to the long term success of your lean program.

When continuing on with your program you can first go through the entire manufacturing or logistics work centres before going into the office work centres, alternatively you can mix it up and involve different work centres throughout the program.

By mixing things up you are ensuring the entire business becomes involved from a relatively early point in the process. This can help build harmony in the business through the change; especially if you build cross functional teams. You can also bring some of the competition ideas into the program earlier and once again you will bring different parts of the business together from an early point.

By continuing through the manufacturing or logistics areas before going into the offices you will have much better continuity throughout the change process. Starting at the end process and working backwards through the business process you will create a demand for positive change as you go. This is explained in detail in the book 7 Steps To A Lean Business – in short, when a process goes through any positive change, it will be more demanding of the upstream process to feed it with improved quality and increased efficiency. This demand will create more urgency to continue the journey.

I have always favoured the second option above of completing the 5S program in one area before progressing backwards simply because of the demand for change that come about. There is no real right or wrong way to proceed so whichever you are more comfortable with and best suits your needs is the way you should go about it.

To achieve sustainability it is critical this ongoing 5S program be managed by the business and not by a facilitator. This is probably the most critical success factor to achieving sustainability. An effective training and handover are far more important than the results of the first 5S run. If you are relying on the facilitator for every review, only a small number can be undertaken at a time. However if the ownership lies with the management team every department can continuously review their own areas. This is true for all Lean Business Tools.

Appendix A – Bonus Schemes

Many organisations incorporate bonus schemes into their remuneration package. These schemes can apply to all departments of a business and can be applied to both salaried and hourly staff. There can be many benefits to the use of bonus schemes including:

- Greater ownership of outcomes

- Performance (results) driven employees

- Self managing team environment

On the other hand, poor bonus schemes can also force employees to focus on insignificant performance targets and can stifle innovation and creativity.

It is quite important to create a positive culture before implementing a bonus scheme rather than implementing a bonus scheme to help create the positive culture. A positive working culture is based on honesty and trust - from all levels of the organisation. Many business owners complain of disloyalty from employees when they do not show any trust, loyalty or empowerment to those same employees. Remember how valuable your employees are to your business. Without them, you would usually not be where you are today.

Back to bonus schemes; there are many different types of schemes. Some are more suitable to certain industries and business types. A quick search on the internet brings up pages of relevant information of the different types of bonus schemes and their pros and cons.

Just remember, a bonus scheme is not a replacement for a strong positive working culture.

Appendix B – The Culture Change

What is a business culture?

There are many definitions of company culture; I like F. John Reh's definition : "A culture is the values and practices shared by the members of the group. Company Culture, therefore, is the shared values and practices of the company's employees." The key word in this statement is "practices"; a culture is really defined by the practices of the group and the practised values. In an organisation the written values and the practised values can differ; sometimes greatly. It is important to identify both.

So to change an organisational culture it is important to not only talk about values and practices but also to live them. For this to happen the people who make up the organisation (employees) need to believe in the values. In many businesses the corporate values will be thought up by the senior management team and then forced down the chain of command throughout the organisation. Because there is no buy-in or belief from the employees this rarely works effectively.

You cannot rush through a culture change in any group and it is even more difficult in an organisation. This is due to the varying personal values the employees all bring to the business. These personal values will mold together to form the company culture.

So how do you go about creating a cultural change? This answer is far too big a question for the appendix of this book however there are many books available on how this process can be managed.

Here are a couple of tips to get you going:

- Develop corporate values through workshops – include as many employees in this process as practicable
- Develop team values through similar process
- Ensure consensus on the values has been gained – encourage constructive debate and discussion
- Empower all employees to "own" the values
- Encourage "values policing" in a positive manner
  - Encourage team members to hold others accountable
- Review values and practices annually to ensure alignment still exists

The change has been adopted when the practices align closely with the values and the new way becomes the new "this is how we've always..." statement.

I feel it is important to restate this appendix is not a guide to creating a culture change in an organisation. It is an overview of what culture is and how it is possible to create a shift in a culture over time.

Appendix C - Tools

Training Material

You have an area to work with; you have buy-in from both parties. Now you need to start training the team. Depending on what stage your business is at with its lean journey this will either be an easy step or a difficult one. There are 5S training programs you can buy "off the shelf" and many of these are quite good. If you are a beginner to implementing 5S you could do worse than buying one of these packages. You could do better though; many local government departments facilitate or sponsor business improvement groups and some of these regularly run training and awareness sessions. Visiting facilities (networking) that have successfully implemented 5S is another good way to gain insights.

While everybody has a different learning style, many people learn best through doing. So whatever training materials and method you select, keep this in mind and try to include as much practical application and activities. There are many activities and games available through stores and online to assist with achieving the "aha!" moment.

While the training material is obviously an important factor in the success of your program, the trainer or facilitator you choose is of greater importance. Select a facilitator with a proven track record. Their success as a trainer or facilitator is probably just as, if not more important than their knowledge of the topic.

Posters and Promotion

Don't be afraid to actively promote every program you run within your organisation. Promotion within the team can improve participation and ownership of the projects. Cross promotion of projects to other work areas can help create a culture of continuous improvement and can also develop a powerful and positive competitive vibe within the organisation. Many leading companies hold regular continuous improvement challenges with associated reward and recognition programs.

Some individuals and companies shy away from the promotion of activities, I don't see any real negatives that come from promoting a project within the team or across the organisation. If you want to start a positive change in the culture of your business then this is somewhere you can start.

Checklists and Audit sheets

Free checklists and audit sheets are available for download from the Lean-Learnings website. www.lean-learnings.com

There is a selection of different checklist to suit many applications. Alternatively you can create your own checklists or search the internet – there are checklists available online. Many are free however some are charged.

Camera

The advent of digital photography has been a great benefit to process improvement. Gone are the days of taking a roll of photographs, waiting for development only to find you didn't quite capture what you wanted to. Now I often take a couple of hundred photographs for both before and after. It is a good idea to keep all photographs you take – just in case. Take the time to organise everything neatly into appropriate folders (electronic 5S) for later reference.

Digital video is another media that can be used to great effect in a 5S program – or many other continuous improvement activities. This is especially useful when modifying a layout of process flow. By capturing the before and after changes on video it is easy to show the benefits in a way that everyone can understand.

Visual Board

Visual boards are a useful tool for:

- Capturing data
- Building awareness
- Information sharing
- Promotion
- Identification of problems

The layout of a visual board is endlessly customisable to suit your requirements. Some examples of visual board layouts are on the Lean-Learnings website www.lean-learnings.com

References

1. F. John Reh
2. 7 Steps To A Lean Business – Jason Tisbury
3. Dictionary.com
4. The Greatest Secret In The World – Og Mandino
5. The Success System That Never Fails
    - W. Clement Stone

Printed in Great Britain
by Amazon.co.uk, Ltd.,
Marston Gate.